EASY HOME
IMPROVEMENTS

*your
bedroom*

EASY HOME
IMPROVEMENTS

your
bedroom

STEWART WALTON

LEBHAR-FRIEDMAN BOOKS

w York • Chicago • Los Angeles • London • Paris • Tokyo

Lebhar-Friedman Books
425 Park Avenue
New York, NY 10022

First U.S. edition published 2001 by Lebhar-Friedman Books
Copyright © 2000 Marshall Editions Ltd, London, U.K.

Published by Lebhar-Friedman Books
Lebhar-Friedman Books is a company of Lebhar-Friedman, Inc.

Printed and bound in China by Excel Printing.
Originated in Singapore by Pica.

Library of Congress Cataloging-in-Publication Data
on file at the Library of Congress.

ISBN: 0-86730-837-0

Project Editor Guy Croton
Designer Glen Wilkins
Editorial Coordinator Caroline Watson
Photographer Alistair Hughes
Managing Editor Antonia Cunningham
Managing Art Editor Phil Gilderdale
Editorial Director Ellen Dupont
Art Director Dave Goodman
Production Amanda Mackie

Front cover photography: **Simon Kelly/Belle/Arcaid**
Back cover photography: **Alistair Hughes**

Visit our Web site at lfbooks.com

Volume Discounts
This book makes a great gift and incentive. Call (212) 756-5240
for information on volume discounts.

Note

contents

introduction

The state of your bedroom has a direct bearing on the state of
your nightly rest. Life today is more stressful than ever before,
so a good night's sleep in sympathetic surroundings is arguably
more important than it was in the past. One of the most
effective ways to ensure a good night's rest is to furnish and
decorate your bedroom in a way that helps you to relax and
get that rest. If you can personalize the room with your favorite
colors and fabrics at the same time, so much the better.

This book is a treasure chest of imaginative projects and
stylish ideas for improving the room that you spend more time
in than any other. Emulating the contents of top interior and
style magazines, *Easy Home Improvements: Your Bedroom*
offers a host of contemporary furnishings and decor ideas
at a fraction of their cost, whilst looking just as good. Why
spend a fortune on a wardrobe when you can make your own
and adjust its dimensions to suit the size of your room?
Why tolerate everyday fabric patterns, colors, and wall
decorations from the homeware store, when it is so simple
and inexpensive to make them to your own taste? Instead,
why not create your own essential bedroom storage items,
furnishings, and decor and tailor them lovingly to your
unique requirements?

The projects in this book range from mundane yet
attractive items such as a laundry box (pages 10–17) and
blanket chest (pages 18–27), to stylish, eye-catching

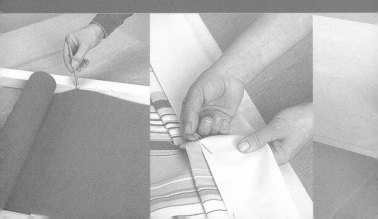

centerpieces like the full-length mirror on pages 54–63. There are practical bedroom aids such as the valet clothes stand on pages 36–43, and more unusual objects like the brightly-colored bedroom screen on pages 90–97. A chapter of bedroom design and decor ideas offers a delightful patchwork throw for your bed, a discreet stencilled lampshade, stylish Roman blinds for your windows, and a classically-patterned stamp to transform even the most drab bedroom wall.

All the projects included in this book were designed to be accessible to as wide a range of people as possible, so none of them are especially difficult to make. Each project is graded with a rough skill rating of "Beginner," "Intermediate," or "Advanced," to help you select the items most suited to your own abilities, backed-up with a rough indication of how long the project should take to make and full details of all the materials and tools required. No specialist skills are needed—the main considerations to keep in mind when making most of these projects are being patient and taking your time. With careful attention to any manufacturer's instructions and standard safety precautions, and the use of good quality tools and protective clothing, you should not encounter any real difficulties in constructing something special and a little different for your bedroom.

Transform your bedroom with this book and get a better night's rest! I hope you get as much satisfaction out of making these projects and practicing the various techniques as I did in preparing them for this book.

Stewart Walton

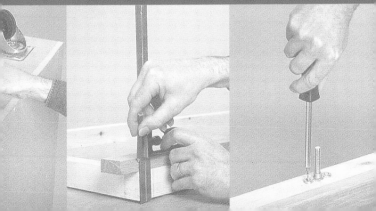

making a **laundry box**

You probably have a laundry basket in your bathroom, but having another one in your bedroom can be very useful. Some people avoid laundry baskets in the bedroom because they are often unsightly, but this stylish, ventilated box overcomes the problem and offers an interesting and attractive variation on the standard wicker baskets you can buy in any home furnishings store.

Materials (all lumber is softwood unless otherwise stated)

Lid: 1 piece of lumber 1 x 8 x 11½ in.

Top of box: 2 pieces of lumber 2 x 1 x 15 in.; 2 pieces of lumber 1 x 2 x 11½ in.

Bottom: 1 piece of plywood ½ x 9½ x 12½ in.

Sides: 2 pieces of lumber 1 x 10½ x 25½ in.

Back and Front: 2 pieces of lumber 1 x 14 x 25½ in.

Battens: 4 pieces of lumber 2 x 1 x 12 in.

Plinth: 4 pieces of lumber 1 x 3¾ x 16 in.

Wooden knob • 2 in. panel pins • Wood glue • Wood filler • Small tin of wax polish • Soft cloth

Tools

Workbench • Power drill with ½ in. bit • Miter saw • Hammer • Nail punch • Tape measure • Rule • Carpenter's pencil • Filling knife • Fine-grade abrasive paper/sanding block

Skill level

Intermediate

Time

8 hours

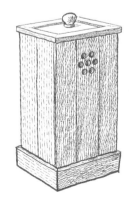

1 Measure and cut all the pieces to the dimensions given in the list of materials. Lay the front and back pieces on the workbench. Position a cut-off piece of wood of the same thickness as the side pieces along the length of the front and back pieces in turn. Take the four battens and mark their positions on the top and bottom of the front and back pieces, 1 in. in from the side edges and ½ in. up from the shorter, end edges.

2 Use a hammer and six panel pins to attach each batten to the front and back pieces in turn. The spaces left at each edge and end allow for the thickness of the side, top, and bottom pieces to be attached to the front and back.

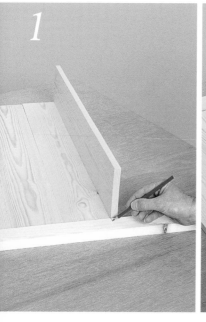

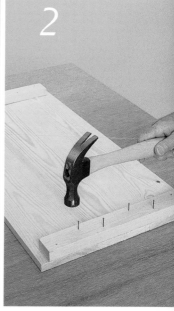

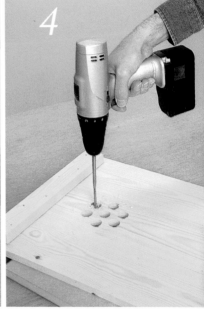

Use a hammer and nail punch to recess the heads of all the panel pins, so that the pins do not protrude and snag on clothes or fingers. Prepare both side pieces in the same way by repeating steps 1–3.

Lay the front and back pieces on the workbench again, with the battens facing upward. Measure and mark a central point on both pieces, 8 in. down from the top edge. Use a power drill and ½ in. bit to drill a hole at this point. Then drill six more holes around the first hole, each about 1 in. from the outer edge of the first hole, in a circular, floral pattern, as shown. These holes will ventilate the laundry box.

5   Once the front, back, and two side pieces have been
    fully prepared, it is time to begin assembling the laundry
    box. Take the two side pieces and stand them on their
    long edges on the workbench. Apply a thin layer of glue
    to the upward edges and the ends of the attached
    battens. Take the back piece and place it over the two
    side pieces so that the edges of the pieces and the
    ends of the battens butt tightly against each other.
    Hammer eight evenly spaced panel pins into each long
    edge of the back piece to attach it to the side pieces.

6   Allow the glue to dry thoroughly and then stand the two
    sides and back piece upright on the workbench. Take
    the bottom piece and fix it in place on top of the lower
    battens, with glue and pins. Repeat step 5 again to
    attach the second side piece.

7 The next step is to measure and cut miter joints into the four pieces of lumber that make up the top of the laundry box. Take each piece in turn and hold it up against the assembled box. Mark the positions of the miter joints at the ends of each piece, where they join the corners of the box. Cut 45-degree miters into the ends of each of the four top pieces, as shown.

8 Glue the mitered top pieces in position on top of the box, with the inner edges ½ in. in from the edges of the upper battens on the inside of the box. The outer edges of the pieces will then extend over the edge of the laundry box, creating a decorative "lip" around it. Use a hammer and four evenly spaced panel pins to secure each of the top pieces in position.

9   The next step is to attach the plinth to the bottom of the box. Hold the four plinth pieces against the box in turn and mark their positions with a pencil. Use the method described in step 7 to mark and cut miters at the ends of each of the four plinth pieces.

10   Glue and pin the plinth pieces in place, so that the plinth protrudes 1 in. below the bottom edges of the box, as shown. Use glue sparingly and hammer evenly spaced panel pins into each plinth piece to attach it to the box.

Helpful hints

Sand off any internal rough edges as you work—especially on the battens—as these will be harder to get to once the laundry box has been assembled.

1 Take the lid of the laundry box and make a pencil mark at its very center. Attach the wooden knob to the middle of the lid, following the manufacturer's instructions. The lid will sit on the recess that you created at the top of the box when you attached the overhanging top pieces in step 8.

2 Fill any gaps in the laundry box as necessary and sand it off until it is smooth, using fine-grade abrasive paper and a sanding block. Then, use a soft cloth and wax polish to bring the box to a pleasing finish.

making a **blanket chest**

Traditional wooden blanket chests have made a comeback in recent years, being practical, spacious and attractive storage items. The only downside is that a really substantial blanket chest can be very expensive to buy, so why not make your own?

Materials (all lumber is softwood unless otherwise stated)

Lid: 1 piece of lumber 1 x 17¼ x 35¼ in. • **Lid edging:** 1 piece of mitered lumber 1 x 1 x 36¼ in. • **Top edging:** 2 pieces of lumber 1 x 3¾ x 15½ in.; 2 pieces of lumber 1 x 3¾ x 34¾ in. • **Bottom:** 1 piece of lumber ½ x 14 x 31¾ in. • **Front and back:** 2 pieces of lumber 1 x 16 x 32 in. • **Sides:** 2 pieces of lumber 1 x 14¼ x 16 in. • **Bottom battens:** 2 pieces of lumber 1 x 2 x 14 in.; 2 pieces of lumber 1 x 2 x 31¾ in. • **Top battens:** 2 pieces of lumber 1 x 2 x 14 in.; 2 pieces of lumber 1 x 2 x 31¾ in. • **Plinth:** 2 pieces of lumber 1 x 3¾ x 15½ in.; 2 pieces of lumber 1 x 3¾ x 34¾ in. • **Backstop:** 1 piece of lumber 1 x 1 x 16½ in. • 36 in. length of rope • Two 2 in. brass hinges • No. 6 (2 in.) screws • 2 in. panel pins • Wood glue • Wood filler

Tools

Workbench • Power drill with ½ in., ⅛ in., screw, and countersinking bits • Hammer • Nail punch • Tape measure • Rule • Carpenter's pencil • Filling knife • Fine-grade abrasive paper/ sanding block

Skill level

Intermediate

Time

8 hours

1 Measure and cut all the pieces to the dimensions given in the list of materials. Lay the front and back pieces in turn flat on the workbench. Take a long bottom batten and hold it along the length of either the front or back. Stand two off-cuts of the same thickness as the front piece at its ends (as shown). Mark the length of the bottom batten from the inside edges of each of the two offcuts. Repeat the process with the other piece and long bottom batten.

2 Use a hammer and fourteen evenly spaced panel pins to attach the bottom batten to the inside of the front piece, ½ in. up from its bottom edge and 1 in. in at each end. Use a nail punch to recess the heads of all the panel pins. Repeat the process with the back piece and long bottom batten.

3   The next step is to measure and attach the top battens
to the outsides of the front and back of the blanket
chest. Repeat the process described in step 1, this time
marking the length of the batten at the *outside* edges of
the off-cuts standing at each end of the front and back.
Unlike the bottom battens, the top battens are positioned
externally and must protrude 1 in. (the thickness of the
board) at each end of the front and back.

4   Repeat the process described in step 2 to attach the
top battens to the front and back, this time hammering
six evenly spaced panel pins into each batten through
the piece from its inside. Ensure that the battens
extend 1 in. on either side, as shown.

5 Prepare the side pieces of the blanket chest following
precisely the same method as described in steps 1–4.
Use a hammer and nail punch to recess the heads of all
the panel pins, as shown. This will prevent blankets and
fingers from snagging on the pin heads.

6 Hold the side pieces up against the ends of either the
front or back on the workbench. Use a power drill and
⅛ in. bit to drill four pilot holes—two at the top, one at
the bottom and one in the middle—through the side
piece and into the end pieces, as shown. Repeat the
process at the other end and with the other side piece.
Countersink all the pilot holes.

7 Use No. 6 (2 in.) screws to attach the side pieces to the front and back through the pilot holes that you drilled in step 6. Hold the pieces square with one another as you drill the screws in. Drill straight into the pilot holes and do not let the screws break through the side pieces.

8 Once the carcass of the blanket chest has been assembled, stand it on the workbench. Take one of the side plinth pieces and position it under the chest, with 2 in. of the plinth piece protruding from the edge, as shown. Use a power drill and ⅛ in. bit to drill three evenly spaced pilot holes—one at each end and one in the middle—through the internal bottom batten and into the plinth piece. Use a thin layer of wood glue and No. 6 (2 in.) screws to attach the side plinth pieces to the bottom of the chest.

9 Repeat the process described in step 8 to prepare and attach the two longer plinth pieces to the bottom of the chest. Again, use wood glue sparingly and four evenly spaced No. 6 (2 in.) screws to make the joints. Wipe away any excess glue immediately with a damp cloth.

10 The carcass is now complete, with a full plinth and top edging. The next step is to secure the bottom of the chest in place. Take the bottom piece and hammer panel pins part-way through it all around its edges. Use four panel pins along the front and back edges and two along the side edges. Place the chest on the workbench and lower the bottom in, seating it on the internal bottom battens attached to the ends and sides in steps 2–5. Reach into the chest and hammer the panel pins firmly into the battens to secure the bottom in place.

1 Take the two brass hinges and use screws to attach them to the back top edge of the chest, positioning each one 6 in. from the end. Hold the lid in position against the chest and then screw the other sides of the hinges to its back edge.

2 Take the backstop and position it centrally on the top back edge of the chest, just beneath the bottom edge of the lid. Lift the lid to ensure that the backstop will prevent it from falling back. Once you are satisfied that the backstop is in the correct position, use a thin layer of wood glue and No. 6 (2 in.) screws to attach the backstop to the chest.

13 Take the lid-edging piece and hold it in position against the front edge of the lid. Use a hammer and five or six evenly spaced panel pins to attach the lid-edging to the front of the lid.

14 Use a hammer and nail punch to recess the heads of the pins in the lid edging. It is important to do this so that sharp points do not protrude from the part of the chest that will be handled most frequently.

Helpful hints

Lay the chest on blocks of off-cut wood on the workbench as you attach the lid edging, so that it is not balancing on the backstop as you hammer in the panel pins.

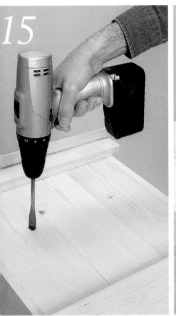

Measure and mark two fixing points for the rope
handles at each side of the chest. These should be
positioned centrally at each end, 6 in. or so down from
the top of the chest and 6 in. apart from one another.
Use a power drill with a ½ in. bit to drill two holes for
each rope handle, as shown.

Cut an 18 in. length of rope for each handle. Tie a knot
6 in. from each end of the rope. Thread each end
through a hole from the outside of the chest and tie a
second knot in the ends of the rope inside the chest.
This way there will be a knot in the rope handles on
both sides of the end pieces, that will hold the handles
firmly in place. Fill and sand the chest as necessary, and
wax, varnish, or paint it as you wish.

making an
open-unit wardrobe

A wardrobe is often one of the most expensive pieces of furniture that you will buy, and many of those available have a disappointing tendency to be either too small or the wrong shape. Make your own wardrobe or box unit, and you can customize it to your own specific needs. This is a versatile and stylish item of furniture that is relatively straightforward to construct, made from inexpensive materials.

Materials

Base: 1 piece of MDF ¾ x 24 x 37½ in.
Top: 1 piece of MDF ¾ x 24 x 37½ in.
Sides: 2 pieces of MDF ¾ x 24 x 54 in.
Back: 1 piece of MDF ¾ x 37½ x 54 in.
Divider: 1 piece of MDF ¾ x 20 x 52½ in.
Shelves: 2 pieces of MDF ¾ x 15¼ x 20 in.
Rail: 1 piece of dowel 1½ x 20 in.
No. 6 (1½ in.) screws • Wood glue • 4 x 2½-in. deep castors

Tools

• Workbench • Hand saw • Tape measure • Set-square/combination square • Carpenter's pencil • Power drill with 1½ in., ⅛ in., ½ in., screw, and countersinking bits • Hammer • Rule • Abrasive paper/sanding block

Skill level
Advanced

Time
8 hours

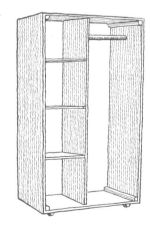

Easy home improvements

1 Lay one of the side pieces flat on the workbench. Hold a piece of ¾ in. MDF board against the side piece, flush with its bottom edge. Draw fixing guidelines for the bottom piece along the edge of the board. Repeat the process at the other end of the side piece, marking fixing guidelines for the top piece.

2 Repeat the process described in step 1 with the other side piece, but this time also mark the positions of the three shelves. Measure 12 in. down from the top edge of the side piece and use the thickness of one of the shelves to mark its position in pencil. Measure and mark the positions of the other two shelves, with a distance of 12 in. between each one. Butt the divider piece against this side piece, aligning the corner with the position of the base of the wardrobe. Use a long rule to draw the shelf position guides onto the divider.

Lay the top piece on the workbench and mark the position of the divider onto it. Use one of the shelves to measure the width from the edge of the top piece and then pencil in the lines by using the thickness of the shelf. The divider should sit centrally along the depth of the wardrobe. Repeat these markings on the bottom piece.

The next step is to mark, drill, and countersink clearance fixing holes in the top, bottom, divider, side pieces, and shelves. These should be evenly spaced and centered in the fixing guidelines drawn in steps 1–3. The shelves will require fixing with two screws at each end and all other pieces with at least three screws at each end. Drill all the clearance holes using a ⅛ in. drill bit. Turn each piece over and countersink the holes from the other side. This leaves the pencil marks on the insides and means that you don't have to transfer the marks to the other side.

5 The wardrobe rail will be attached to the divider and the right-hand side piece (the one without the shelves attached). Mark its fixing positions on both these pieces. Measure halfway along the widths of both pieces and then measure 5 in. down from the top of both pieces. Drill and countersink these two holes, as before. It is very important that the two holes are located in exactly the same position and are level, or the rail will cause assembly problems and will be crooked.

6 Cut four lengths of 2 x 2 in. lumber to the depth of the wardrobe (24 in). Use glue sparingly and No. 6 (2½ in.) screws to fix these along the inside top and bottom edges of the two side pieces to act as corner supports for the base and top. Using glue and screws will make the joints stronger and the overall structure sturdier.

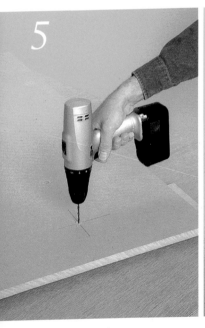

7 Assemble the outer carcass of the wardrobe. Lie the side and the bottom pieces on their sides on the floor. Glue sparingly along the edge of the corner support you attached in step 6 and press the two pieces together. Hold them together and drill $\frac{1}{2}$ in. pilot holes into the bottom piece through the pre-drilled clearance holes in the side piece. Screw the two together, just to hand tightness. Repeat the process with the top and other side pieces. Once the carcass is assembled, tighten up all the screws. Check that everything is square.

8 Lie the carcass flat on the floor. Place the inside divider in position. Also place the shelves in position to ensure that they will butt tightly after final assembly. Glue and screw the divider into position through the clearance holes in the top and bottom, using the same method as before.

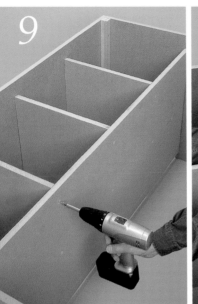

9 Once the divider is in place use the same technique as described in steps 6 and 7 to glue and screw the three shelves into position. Use small blocks of wood to support the shelves as you are screwing them into position. Check frequently that everything is level and square. Stand the wardrobe up.

10 Take the length of dowel to make the wardrobe rail and hold it against the side of the wardrobe. Ensure that you hold it square to the side piece and mark the length where it meets the inside of the divider piece. Cut the dowel to the correct size using a hand saw. Then, fix it in place using No. 6 (1½ in.) screws through the clearance holes that you drilled in the side piece and the divider in step 4.

1 Use coarse abrasive paper and a sanding block to round off the corners of the 2 x 2 in. corner supports. Bring them to a smooth finish. It is essential to do this to prevent anyone catching themselves on the sharp corners. Do this for all eight corners, top, bottom, front, and back.

2 Stand the wardrobe upside down and mark the positions of the castors on its bottom piece. Attach the four castors to the wardrobe following the manufacturer's instructions. Most castors will need to be bolted to the wardrobe, as shown. Fill, sand, and paint or varnish the wardrobe, according to your preference.

making a
valet clothes stand

This free-standing valet clothes stand is made from beech or ash and features a stylishly-shaped top and decorative wooden ball. It will stand anywhere in the bedroom and is discreet and space-efficient enough for the most compact room.

Materials

Uprights: Two pieces of PAR timber measuring 2 x 2 x 40 in.

Top piece: One piece of PAR timber measuring 2 x 6 x 15 in.

Bottom cross pieces: Four pieces of oak measuring 1½ x 1½ x 17¾ in.

Feet: Two pieces of PAR timber measuring 1½ x 5 x 9½ in.

Pants rail: One piece of dowel measuring 1 x 15 in.

2½ in.-diameter wooden ball with embedded screw in base •
No. 8 (3 in.) screws • Wood glue • Small tin of wax polish, varnish, or paint

Tools

Workbench • Power drill with ¼ in., ⅛ in., screw, and countersinking bits • Jigsaw •
Tape measure • Rule •
Carpenter's pencil • Fine-grade
abrasive paper/sanding block •
Soft cloth • Brush • Paint brush •
Wooden coat hanger

Skill level

Beginner

Time

4 hours

Easy home improvements

1 Measure and cut all the pieces to the dimensions given in the list of materials. Take the top piece and lay it on the workbench. Take a sturdy wooden coat hanger and lay it over the top piece. Use a pencil to trace the shape of the coat hanger onto the top piece. Clamp the top piece into the workbench. Use a jigsaw to cut out the sloping "shoulders" of the top piece, as shown.

2 Lay the cut-out top piece flat on the workbench. Take the two uprights and lay them alongside the top pieces so that their top ends butt against the ends of the top piece. Use a pencil and rule to mark the angle of the sloping shoulders of the top piece across the tops of the uprights, as shown. Clamp the uprights into the workbench and use the jigsaw to cut along the pencil lines.

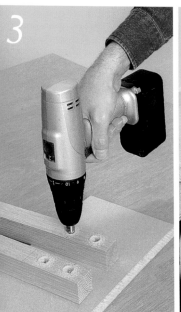

3 Mark two evenly spaced vertical fixing points on the top
ends of the uprights where they will join the ends of
the top piece. Drill clearance holes at the four fixing
points using a ¼ in. bit. Countersink the four holes.

4 Lay the top piece on the workbench with the two
uprights in position alongside. Butt the pieces together
so that the angled ends of the uprights align perfectly
with the sloping shoulders of the top piece. Use a ⅛ in.
bit to drill pilot holes into the ends of the top piece
through the clearance holes that you drilled in step 3.
Attach the uprights to the top piece with a thin layer of
glue and No. 8 (3 in.) screws.

5 Take the four bottom cross pieces and place them on the workbench. Mark a fixing point at both ends of each piece, centered and ½ in. in from the end. Use a ¼ in. bit to drill clearance holes through the cross pieces at each marked point. Countersink all the holes.

6 Take the two feet and place them upright on the workbench. Lay the first bottom cross piece across the two feet, so that the ends of the feet butt squarely with the ends of the cross piece. Use a combination square to ensure that it is properly in position. Repeat the process with the second cross piece at the other end of the feet. Drill ¼ in. pilot holes into the tops of the feet through the clearance holes that you drilled in the cross pieces in step 5. Attach the first two cross pieces to the feet with a little glue and No. 8 (3 in.) screws.

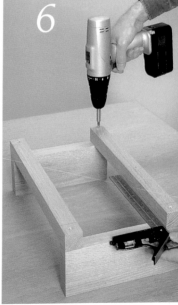

7 The two uprights of the valet clothes stand will be attached centrally on the foot stand. To mark their fixing positions, take the remaining two bottom cross pieces and butt them together against one of the fixed cross pieces, as shown. Draw a line across the top of both feet at the outside edge of the butted cross pieces. Repeat the process at the other end of the feet. The pencil lines will accurately indicate the fixing positions for the two uprights.

8 The next step is to attach the two uprights to the sides of one of the remaining bottom cross pieces. This is necessary to give the uprights extra support. Butt the ends of the uprights squarely with those of the cross piece and mark, drill, and secure the pieces as before, following the process described in step 6.

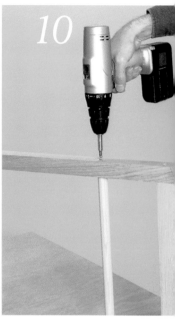

9 Take the assembled frame of the two uprights and one bottom cross piece and hold it up against the two feet and their attached cross pieces. Position the bottom of the uprights in the fixing guidelines that you marked in step 7. Drill ⅛ in. pilot holes into the tops of the feet through the two clearance holes in the ends of the bottom cross piece. Attach the cross piece to the feet, once again using a little glue and No. 8 (3 in.) screws to make the joint. Attach the fourth and last cross piece using the same method, but also butt it tightly up against the uprights and secure it to them with a little glue.

10 Take the piece of dowel for the pants rail and hold it in position 6 in. down from the top of the two uprights. Ensure that it is level and fitted squarely. Mark its position, drill pilot holes, glue, and screw the rail to the uprights using the method described in step 6.

1. Lay the clothes stand on its side on the workbench. Measure and mark a point at the center of the top piece, on its top edge. Drill a ⅛ in. pilot hole ½ in. deep into the top piece. The wooden ball that you attach to decorate the clothes stand will have a fixing screw embedded in it. Apply a little glue to the bottom of the ball around this screw and then screw the ball onto the top piece by hand.

2. Finish the clothes stand by sanding the entire unit smooth with fine-grade abrasive paper and a sanding block. Dust off the clothes stand with a brush, and wax, varnish, or paint as you wish.

chapter 2
Furniture

making a
night table

This table features a useful low shelf on which to keep bedtime reading. Inexpensive and easy to construct, it does not take long to make and can be painted or varnished to match the decor and other furnishings in your bedroom. If you make two, they look very attractive on either side of a double bed.

Materials (all lumber is softwood unless otherwise stated

Top: 1 piece of MDF ¾ x 16 x 16 in.

Shelf: 1 piece of MDF ¾ x 16 x 16 in.

Shelf supports: 2 pieces of PAR 1 x 1 x 16 in.

Legs: 4 pieces of PAR 2 x 2 x 24 in.

Edging pieces: 8 pieces of PAR ¼ x 1¾ x 16⅝ in.

No. 6 (1½ in.) screws • 1 in. panel pins • Wood glue • Wood filler • Paint or varnish • Paint brushes

Tools

Workbench • Hand saw • Miter saw • Tape measure • Set-square/combination square • Carpenter's pencil • Power drill with ⅛-in., ½ in., screw, and countersinking bits • Hammer • Nail punch • Rule • Filling knife • Abrasive paper/sanding block

Skill level

Intermediate

Time

4 hours

Easy home improvements

1   Lay the shelf piece flat on the workbench. Take the four legs and stand one at each corner. Ensure that the ends of the legs are square to the shelf and use a pencil to mark their positions on it. These lines mark the areas of the shelf that will be cut away to accommodate the legs.

2   Draw the four sets of leg guidelines over onto the thickness of the shelf piece to facilitate cutting out the excess wood. Clamp the shelf firmly and squarely into the workbench. Use a hand saw to cut out the four waste wood pieces. Saw carefully, ensuring that your cut lines are straight and square with each other.

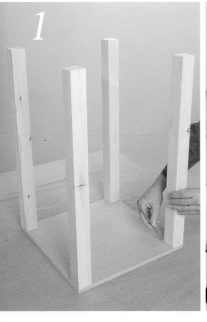

3 To mark out the positions for the two shelf supports on each of the four legs, butt the four legs together on the workbench, using a straight piece of wood to press against the bottom edges. When the four legs are accurately butted together, use a pencil to mark across all four legs 6 in. up from the bottom edges. Use a set-square to ensure that this line will be perfectly level with the floor on the finished piece.

4 Take the two shelf support pieces and mark off the width of a leg against the end of each one. Use a square and a rule to mark the positions of two evenly spaced clearance fixing holes on each end of the shelf supports, inside the fixing guidelines for the legs. Carefully drill the clearance holes in each end of the two shelf supports, using a ⅛ in. drill bit.

5 Hold each of the shelf supports in position with a leg
against it at each end. Drill reciprocal pilot holes into the
legs through the clearance holes that you drilled into the
shelf supports in step 4, using a ½ in. bit. Apply a thin
layer of glue to all joints and then fix the shelf supports
to the legs, using No. 6 (1½ in.) screws. Use a set-
square to ensure that the supports are square to each
of the legs.

6 Hold the shelf in position against the assembled legs
and shelf supports. Carefully mark evenly spaced fixing
positions for the two supports onto the four corners of
the shelf. Drill a ⅛ in. pilot hole into each corner of the
shelf, as shown. Ensure that you drill straight and square
to the shelf. Countersink the pilot holes, to hide the
screw heads when the shelf is screwed into position.

7 Stand the two sets of assembled legs and shelf supports up on the workbench. Check once more that the shelf fits snugly into position. Carefully glue the shelf where it butts against the supports and against the legs themselves. Screw the shelf into position, making sure the screws bite into the supports and that everything is straight and square.

8 Place the top piece in position over the table legs and carefully mark fixing positions to attach it to the legs. The table top should be secured with two screws into each leg. Drill and countersink pilot holes as described in step 6. Glue and screw the top onto the four legs. Check at every stage that the top is level and that the table sits square and even on the floor.

9   Cut an edging piece to a length 2 in. wider than the
table top. Hold the edging piece up against the top
edge of the table. Mark the positions of 45-degree miter
joints at the ends of the edging piece. Repeat this
process for all eight edging pieces.

10   Use a miter saw to cut 45-degree miters at the ends of
all eight edging pieces. Check the fit of the edging
pieces against the table and smooth off their ends with
abrasive paper wrapped around a sanding block.

Helpful hints

*The dimensions of PAR timber often vary slightly, so be
careful to match different pieces to one another at the
outset of this project and keep them together throughout.*

1 Once the pieces are all mitered and you are satisfied with their fit, attach them to the table by glueing and then pinning them. Use a hammer and five 1 in. evenly spaced panel pins to attach each edging piece.

2 Use a nail punch to recess the pin heads in the surfaces of the edging pieces. Ensure that all the edging pieces are fitted squarely and evenly, and that they butt together tightly at the corners. Use wood filler and a flexible filling knife to fill any gaps in the miters or elsewhere, as well as over all the countersunk screwheads. Sand to a smooth finish and paint or varnish according to your taste.

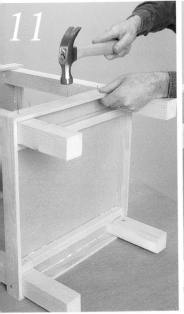

making a
full-length mirror

A full-length mirror is a very useful item in the bedroom, particularly if it is free-standing and you can adjust the angle to suit yourself.

Materials (all lumber is softwood unless otherwise stated)

Mirror: 21 x 51 in.

Mirror frame uprights: Two pieces of PAR timber 2 x 1½ x 54 in.

Cross pieces: Two pieces of PAR timber 2 x 1½ x 24 in.

Side struts: Two pieces of PAR timber 2 x 2 x 36 in.

Bottom strut: One piece of PAR timber 2 x 2 x 24 in.

Feet: Two pieces of PAR timber 3 x 2 x 36 in.

Backboard: One piece of ply ½ x 20 x 48 in.

Oak facing: Length of oak ½ x 1½ in. x 14 ft.

Battens: Two pieces of PAR timber 1 x 1 x 51 in.; two pieces of PAR timber 1 x 1 x 19 in.

Two swivel-fixing bolts (½ in. barrels), brackets, and screws • No. 8 (3 in.) screws • 1½-in. panel pins • Wood glue

Tools

Workbench • Tape measure • Combination square • Hand saw • Miter saw • Pencil • Power drill with ½ in., ⅛ in., ½ in., ⅟₁₆ in. and screw bits • Hammer • Bradawl • Rule • Abrasive paper/block • Brush • Wax polish • Wire wool • Soft cloth

Skill level

Intermediate

Time

4 hours

1 The first stage is to make the frame to hold the mirror. Take the two mirror-frame upright pieces and mark two evenly spaced fixing holes ½ in. in at each end. The frame cross pieces will be attached with screws through these holes. Drill clearance holes using a ⅛ in. bit. Countersink all eight holes.

2 Take the two mirror-frame cross pieces and lay them on the workbench with the two upright pieces. Hold the end of one cross piece up against the side of one end of one of the uprights. Use a combination square to ensure that they butt squarely up against each other. Drill ½ in. reciprocal pilot holes into the ends of the cross pieces through the clearance holes that you drilled in the ends of the uprights in step 1. Attach one cross piece to both uprights using a little glue and No. 8 (3 in.) screws. Repeat this step with the other cross piece.

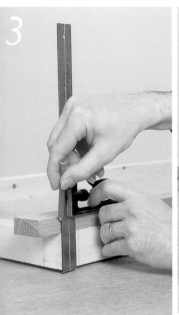

Once the mirror frame has been assembled, the next step is to attach the oak facing. Cut a length of oak 2 in. longer than the frame (56 in.). Butt one end of the oak with the end of the frame and mark a 45-degree miter at the other end with a combination square and pencil where it meets the top edge of the cross piece. Repeat the process at the other end of the oak and for the other frame upright and both cross pieces. Cut all four pieces of oak facing on a miter saw.

The oak facing is attached with 1½ in. panel pins and wood glue. Position it so that its outer edge is flush with the outer edge of the mirror frame. Use glue sparingly to secure the facing pieces to the front of the frame. Then, use a ⅟₁₆ in. drill bit to drill five evenly spaced clearance holes into each upright oak facing and three into the cross piece oak facings.

5 Secure the oak facing to the mirror frame by hammering the panel pins into the frame through the clearance holes that you drilled in the oak facing in step 4. Use a nail punch to press the heads of the panel pins firmly into the oak facing. When the oak facing is in place, its inner edge will protrude slightly over that of the mirror frame, creating a "lip" for the mirror to sit on once the unit is assembled.

6 The next step is to attach the swivel fixing bolts that hold the mirror frame into its base. Measure 28 in. up both outer sides of the mirror frame from its bottom edge. Mark a point in the center of each frame upright. Hold the frame up on its side on the workbench, as shown. Use a ½ in. drill bit to drill a hole halfway through each upright, from its outer side. These holes will accommodate the swivel fixing bolts.

7 Push the barrels of the two swivel fixing bolts into the holes that you drilled in step 6. Follow the manufacturer's instructions to screw the bolts and brackets onto the outer sides of the mirror frame uprights, as shown. You should not need to drill clearance holes for the small bolt screws.

8 The next step is to shape the top of the feet that will be attached to the mirror base. Place the two foot pieces on the workbench. Mark a point 6 in. in from each end on the top edge of each foot. Mark another point 1 in. down from the top edge on each side of both feet. Draw two straight lines between these points on each foot. Clamp each foot in turn into the workbench. Use a hand saw to cut along each line.

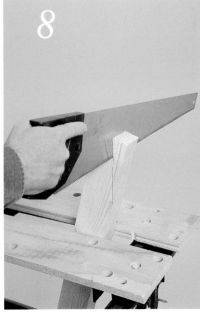

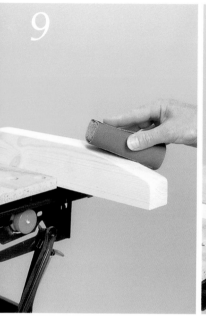

9 When you have cut away the excess wood from the
top of both feet, use coarse abrasive paper and a
sanding block to rub the feet down to a smooth,
rounded-off finish.

10 Take the two side struts that the mirror frame will be
attached to and clamp them horizontally into the
workbench. Measure 7 in. down from their top ends to
mark the positions of the reciprocal fixing holes for the
swivel fixing bolts attached to the mirror frame in step
7. Use a ¼ in. drill bit to drill the fixing holes all the way
through the thickness of the two side struts.

1 Clamp one of the two foot pieces face-up into the workbench. Hold one of the side struts on top of the foot, with its end centered on the width of the flat part of the foot top and flush with its outer edge, as shown. Draw a line around the bottom of the side strut, to mark its fixing position on the top of the foot. Repeat with the other foot and side strut.

2 Drill two evenly spaced ⅛ in. clearance holes within the fixing guidelines marked on the tops of the feet in step 11. Drill all the way through each foot. Hold the feet up against the side struts on the workbench and drill reciprocal ½ in. pilot holes into the bottoms of the side struts through the clearance holes that you have just drilled. Use a little wood glue and 5 in. screws to attach the feet to the side struts.

13 The next step is to assemble the mirror frame and base unit, attaching each of the two sets of side struts and feet to the mirror frame using the swivel fixing bolts that you attached in step 7. Lay the mirror frame and its base down flat on the workbench. Hold the bottom base strut in position between the side struts where they meet the top of the feet. Mark the position of the bottom base strut on the inside of each side strut. Take the unit apart again.

14 Take the mirror frame once more and place it flat on the workbench, with the oak facing upward. Use a soft cloth and wax polish to bring a shiny grain out of the oak facing. Leave the oak facing to dry and then repeat the process, this time using very fine wire wool to rub the wax polish gently into the oak surface.

The next step is to secure the mirror into the frame. Place the mirror in position in the frame and carefully position the ply backboard over it. Take the four lengths of 1 x 1 in. batten, cut to the internal dimensions of the frame (see list of materials). These will secure the mirror and backboard in place. Hold each piece of batten in position inside the mirror frame and secure them by hammering evenly spaced 1½ in. panel pins through the battens and into the inside of the frame.

Use the method described in step 12 to attach the bottom strut to each of the side struts in turn. Complete the final assembly of the mirror and its base by sliding the swivel fixing bolts through the clearance holes in the side struts and attaching the brass wing nuts to the ends of the bolts. Set the mirror to the desired angle in its base and tighten the brass wing nuts.

making an "S"-shaped shelf

This easy-to-make "S"-shaped shelf is a stylish bedroom furnishing that will enhance the look of the items that you put on it. It does not require any special woodworking skills or tools and is probably the least expensive project to make in this book.

Materials

Bottom shelf: 1 piece of lightweight hardwood 2 x 8 x 18¼ in.
Middle shelf: 1 piece of lightweight hardwood 2 x 8 x 18¼ in.
Top shelf: 1 piece of lightweight hardwood 2 x 8 x 8½ in.
Bottom upright: 1 piece of lightweight hardwood 2 x 8 x 10 in.
Top upright: 1 piece of lightweight hardwood 2 x 8 x 10 in.
Shelf edging: cut from length of Parana pine 1 x 1¼ in. x 7 ft.
2 mirror-style brass fixing brackets • No. 6 (1½ in.) screws • Wood glue • Wood filler • Masking tape

Tools

Workbench • Hand saw • Miter saw • Tape measure • Rule • Craft knife • Filling knife • Combination square • Carpenter's pencil • Power drill with ⅛ in., ⅛ in., screw, and countersinking bits • Abrasive paper/block

Skill level

Beginner

Time

4 hours

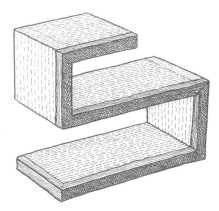

1 Place the top shelf and the top upright beside each other on the workbench. Hold the thickness of the shelf against the upright and draw a fixing guideline across the width of the top upright at both ends. Mark two evenly spaced clearance fixing holes in the center of the pencil guidelines, at the top and bottom of the upright. Use a ⅛ in. drill-bit to drill the clearance holes in the outside of the top upright. When you have finished drilling, countersink the holes.

2 Hold the top upright in position against the top shelf and use a smaller, ⅛ in., drill-bit to drill reciprocal pilot holes into the end of the shelf, through the clearance holes that you drilled in the top upright piece in step 1.

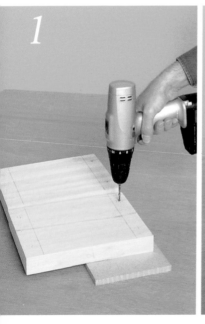

3 Apply wood glue sparingly to the end of the top upright piece to be attached to the top shelf. This will help strengthen the joint that you are about to make with screws. Be careful not to use too much glue and wipe off any excess with a damp cloth.

4 Attach the top upright piece to the top shelf using No. 6 (1½ in.) screws. Repeat steps 1–3 to attach the middle shelf to the other end of the top upright. Next, use the same method to attach the bottom upright to the other end of the middle shelf, so that the "S" shape of the shelf is almost complete.

5 Once you have assembled the two uprights and top and middle shelves, mark the fixing position of the bottom shelf, or base piece. As with all your joints, it is vital that the bottom shelf is connected squarely to the rest of the shelf unit, to ensure that the shelves are level and the unit is sturdy. Repeat steps 1–3 to attach the bottom shelf to the bottom upright and complete the "S" shape of the shelf unit.

6 The next stage is to cut and attach the mahogany shelf facings. Cut a strip of mahogany facing to a length slightly greater than the width of the top shelf. Hold it in position across the width of the shelf. Use a pencil and rule to mark the positions of 45-degree miter joints at each end of the shelf. Repeat the process for all parts of the shelf, on both sides.

7   Use a miter saw to cut 45-degree miter joints into each end of all the mahogany strips. Make precise cuts and then sand off any rough edges on the miters using fine abrasive paper and a block.

8   Once you are satisfied with the lengths and miter joints of the mahogany edging pieces, attach them to the front edges of the unit using wood glue. Apply the glue sparingly and wipe off any excess immediately with a damp cloth. Use strips of masking tape to hold the mahogany edgings in place as the glue dries. Complete the shelf unit by thoroughly filling all the screw holes and any obvious gaps in the joints with wood filler and a flexible filling knife. Wait for the filler to dry, and then sand it off to a smooth finish. Either stand the shelf on a flat surface, or attach brackets to fix it to the wall.

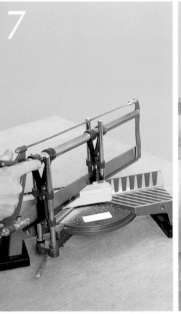

chapter 3
Finishing touches

sewing a
patchwork throw

Traditionally, patchwork quilts were handsewn by women using left-over scraps of material — making the quilt a fabric history of the lives of their family and friends. These days, using an electric sewing machine, the work is much quicker, but you can still make your own personally designed quilt from left-over materials, or to match your bedroom decor, for a fraction of what it would cost you to buy. The measurements for this quilt are for a double bed, and we have chosen a checkerboard design.

Materials

2 yd. each of two different 54-in. width feature fabrics, one plaid and one floral • 2 yd. of 54-in. width backing fabric (green glazed cotton) • 1 yd. contrasting fabric for edging, e.g. pale blue chambray cotton • 1½yd. of 60-in. width quilter's wadding • 1 yd. iron-on wadding for edging strips • Thread

Tools

Electric sewing machine • Tape measure • Steam iron • Fine needle for tacking • Pins • Scissors • 9 in. square of card for template

Skill level

Intermediate

Time

4 hours

1 Cut a 9 in. square out of scrap card or thin board. This
will be used as a template to cut out the squares of
fabric that make up the patchwork on the throw. Use
the template to draw squares onto the fabric. You will
need to mark out an equal number of squares on each
of the two fabrics that you use. For this quilt you will
need forty squares of each fabric (or eighty in total, if
you are using several different materials). The finished
quilt will be 8 x 10 squares in size.

2 Place two squares of each material, pattern sides together
and tack along one of their edges on the "wrong" side of
the material. Take the next alternate square and place it
pattern side down on the pattern side of one of the sewn
squares. Tack and sew. Repeat until you have completed
the row of eight squares. Use this technique to sew each
of the ten rows of alternate fabric squares together.

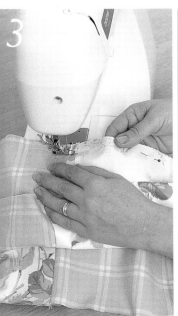 

3 Ensuring that all the squares line up accurately with each other, sew the ten rows together. Sew through the underside of the material so that all the seam edges are on the "wrong" side of the quilt. As you sew, keep checking to ensure that the seams are straight. Sew all ten rows together.

4 Lay out the iron-on wadding on a flat, heat-proof, clean surface and cut it to the same size as the patchwork fabric you have just stitched together (72 x 90 in.). Lay the patchwork fabric over the top of the wadding pattern side up, and ensure that they fit accurately together. Smooth out any creases with your hands. Use a hot steam iron to press the patchwork onto the wadding, following the manufacturer's instructions. The heat of the steam will bond the two fabrics together.

5   Turn the assembled patchwork fabric and wadding over
    and lay the green backing fabric over it. Again, ensure
    that the green backing fabric is cut to exactly the same
    size as the patchwork. Machine sew all around the
    edges, joining the three layers together. Sew all four
    corners and trim away any loose threads or excess
    material from the edges of the squares.

6   To make the edging strips, first measure the length and
    the width of the quilt. Cut four strips of the edging
    material, two for the length and two for the width of the
    quilt. These edging strips should measure 5 in. across.

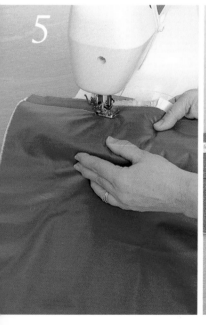

7 Take each edging piece in turn. First fold it in half and then iron it to crease the fold into the material. Now fold a ½ in. hem on either side of the edging. Again, iron this firmly into the material.

8 Cut a strip of the iron-on wadding measuring 2½ in. wide and the length of the quilt (72 in.). Iron this into the inside of one of the edging pieces. Repeat this process for the other three sides/edgings.

Helpful hints

If you are keen to cut costs, it is far cheaper to use regular wadding rather than the iron-on version recommended here, but you will need to sew down the edges.

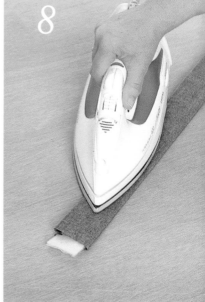

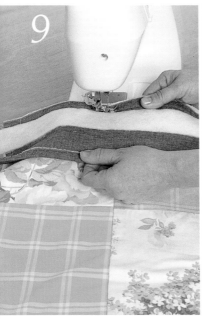

9 When the wadding is bonded firmly into each edging strip, open the edging out and machine sew it to the front edge of the patchwork quilt, with the "good" side of the edging to the "good" side of the quilt. Sew all four edgings onto the quilt in turn, ½ in. in from the edge, ensuring that you sew all the way around in a straight line.

10 Once the edging strips are sewn onto the top of the quilt, carefully fold them over onto the underside of the quilt and pin them into position all the way around.

Helpful hints

Although it is tempting to just pin your fabrics together before sewing them, tacking them will ensure that your seams are as straight as possible.

1 To complete the quilt, begin by hand sewing the corners. The corners of the edging strips should be folded completely flat onto each other. Make the folds as neat as possible, smoothing out any creases, and hand stitch them carefully into place, using a fine needle.

2 To finish off, hand sew the edging on all four sides of the quilt, using a hem stitch. Trim away any loose threads and excess material. Iron the finished quilt thoroughly to smooth out any creases.

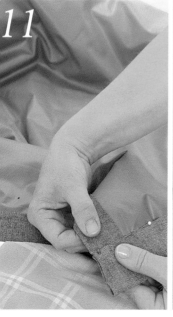

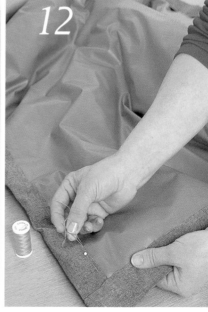

making Roman blinds

Roman blinds make an attractive alternative to curtains in the bedroom. They are not very difficult to make, and require less material than most curtain designs. Additionally, as you can choose your fabrics, patterns, and colors, making them gives you the option of matching your blinds more closely to the decor of your room than if you bought them from a store or catalog.

Materials

Fabric to fit your window—measure drop plus 8 in. and width plus 4 in. • Lining fabric (calico)—actual size of drop and width measurement • 3 (or more) ⅝ in. dowel rods—width of hemmed lining fabric • 2 x 1 in. blind header batten to width of blind • 12 small rings • 3 brass screw-in eyelets • Blind pull • Thread • No. 6 (2 in.) screws • Wall plugs

Tools

Worksurface • Electric sewing machine • Power drill with ¼ in. bit • Spirit level • Steam iron • Pins • Staple gun or tacks and hammer • Double-sided tape • Needle

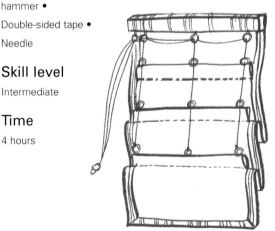

Skill level

Intermediate

Time

4 hours

Easy home improvements

1 Place the fabric for the blind face down on your work-surface. Measure and turn over a 2 in. seam along both sides of the fabric and along the bottom edge. Use a hot steam iron to press along the edge of the seam so that it remains in place (as shown). To fold the corners of the fabric into neat miters, fold the bottom right- and left-hand corners diagonally inward along the point where the side and bottom folds intersect. Then fold the side seam over and the bottom seam over so that the edges butt against each other. Iron the seams and corners flat.

2 Repeat the process on the lining fabric, turning and pressing a ½ in. hem into the edges of the calico. Then, place the lining fabric face-up on top of the blind fabric. Pin the lining fabric carefully into position over the wrong side of the fabric for the blind.

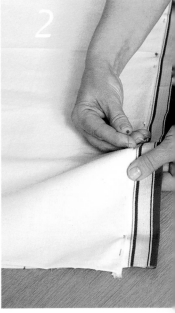

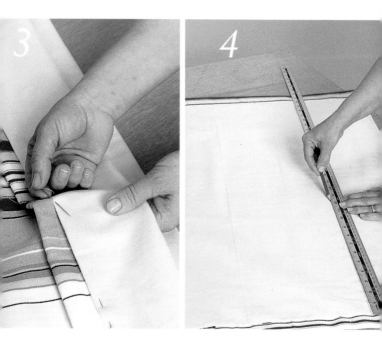

3 Attach the lining fabric to the fabric for the blind. Do this
by hand slip-stitching along all four edges of the lining
material. Ensure that the hemmed edges of the lining
fabric and the blind fabric align correctly as you sew.

4 The next step is to decide upon the positions of the
dowel tubes on the blind and the distances of drop
between them. Measure the overall required drop length
of the blind from the bottom hem upward and draw a
line centrally along the length of the blind. Divide the
drop length into several equal sections. In this case, the
total drop length is 42 in. The line for the lowest and
highest section is drawn 9 in. from the top and bottom
edges of the blind, with two others between them
marked at 12 in. intervals, making up the overall drop
length of 42 in.

5 Cut out three pieces of calico fabric to make up the dowel tubes (more, if your blind is longer than the one featured in this project). These should be cut to the width of the lining fabric x 4 in. Fold the calico dowel tube pieces in half lengthways and press them with a hot steam iron. Then, press a ½ in. hem onto both the raw edges of each piece of material.

6 Fold in one end of each of the calico dowel tubes. Use a sewing machine to stitch along it and along the entire length of the tube, leaving the other end of the tube open and un-stitched. The open ends of the calico tubes will receive the dowel rods as you begin assembling the blind.

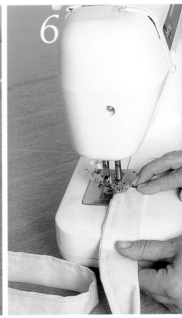

7   When you have made all the calico dowel tubes, stitch each one of them to the blind fabric along the pencil lines drawn to mark the positions of each one in step 4. Machine stitch along the length of each dowel tube, just inside the folded edge. Make sure that they are straight and that the thread matches the material of the blind, as these lines of stitching will be visible on the good side of the blind.

8   Each dowel tube will have several stringing rings/eyelets attached to it (in this case, three). Measure 4 in. in from each end of the attached dowel tubes to mark the positions of the outer rings. Halve the distance between the outer rings to ascertain the position of the middle one. Use the same method to calculate the positions of any further rings needed. Hand sew the brass rings onto the double-sewn seam edge of the dowel tubes.

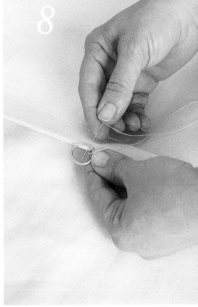

9 Measure and trim the dowel pieces to ½ in. short of the tube lengths, and insert one dowel piece into each tube on the blind.

10 When the dowels are all in place, slip-stitch the ends of the calico tubes to close them. The hanging framework of the Roman blind is now in place.

Helpful hints

When fixing the header batten to the blind, it is essential to keep the batten square to the edge of the fabric in order for the blind to pull up straight.

1 Cut a scrap of excess blind fabric in two and use the pieces to cover the ends of the blind header batten. Use double-sided tape to hold the scraps of cloth in position over the batten ends, and then secure the wrapped-over edges of cloth to the batten using a staple gun.

2 Place the blind rolled-out flat on the worksurface. Take the header batten and align it carefully with the top end of the blind. Roll the batten over twice into the fabric, so that the end of the blind wraps around it. Use a staple gun to secure the blind to the header batten, punching evenly-spaced staples into the fabric along the entire back edge of the batten.

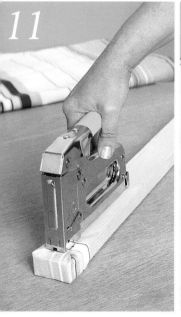

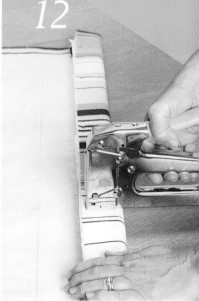

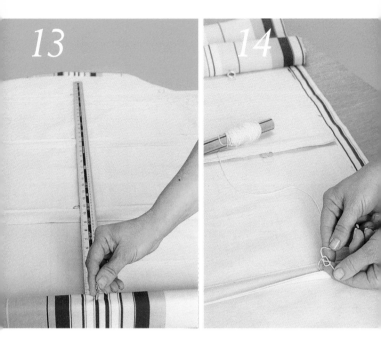

13 Position three screw-in eyelets on the underside of the batten so that they line up with the brass rings that you attached to the dowel tubes in step 8. Screw one additional brass eyelet through the material 1 in. in from the edge of the batten where the cord is to hang.

14 The blind is operated by three separate cords. Decide which side of the blind you want the cords to operate from. Then tie one end of the first cord to the lowest ring on the opposite side of the blind.

Helpful hints

Use the same procedure to make un-lined Roman blinds, if you would prefer to filter rather than block out the light shining through your window.

5 Thread the first cord up through the first line of rings, above then across all the eyelets, and allow a drop length in the cord of about two-thirds of the length of the blind. Repeat the process with the other two cords, threading them through the other two vertical sets of rings and across the top of the blind in the same way.

6 Finally, thread all three cord ends through the top of the pull that you will use to lower and raise the blind. Trim the ends of all three cords to precisely the same length and tie them in a neat knot. Your Roman blind is now ready for fixing to the wall. Drill a hole 1 in. in from each end of the header batten and use No. 6 (2 in.) screws and wall plugs to attach the blind to the wall above the window. Use a spirit level to ensure that the blind header batten is level.

making a
three-panel screen

A screen is a time-honored bedroom furnishing traditionally used for dressing behind or for dividing up a room—particularly when more than one person or couple is sleeping in it. This good-looking screen is made from wood and canvas and is easy to put together. It is not too large, so it will fit into any size bedroom. The screen has three folding sections, so it can be easily stored away when it is not in use.

Materials (all lumber is softwood unless otherwise stated)

Panel uprights: Six pieces of PAR timber measuring 2 x 1½ x 60 in.

Dowel cross pieces: Twelve pieces of dowel measuring ¾ x 17¼ in.

Roll of canvas measuring 17½ x 200 in.

Six brass hinges • No. 8 (2½ in.) brass screws and screw cups • No. 6 (1 in.) brass screws and screw cups • Brass, round-headed panel pins • Double-sided adhesive tape

Tools

Workbench • 2 G-clamps • Tape measure • Combination square • Hand saw • Miter saw • Pencil • Power drill with ⅛ in., ⅛ in., ½ in., screw, and countersinking bits • Hammer • Bradawl • Rule • Abrasive paper/sanding block • Brush

Skill level

Intermediate

Time

4 hours

1 The screen consists of three panels, each comprising two uprights and three cross braces. Butt two of the panel uprights together on their narrow edges on the workbench. Hold each cross brace in position against the uprights and draw pencil guidelines along either side. The bottom cross brace should be positioned 2 in. up from the bottom of the uprights. The top cross brace should be positioned flush with the top end. The middle cross brace should be positioned 18 in. down from the top of the uprights. Repeat the process with the other two sets of uprights and cross braces.

2 Draw a diagonal line across each of the cross brace fixing guidelines and mark two evenly spaced points on the line. Use a ⅛ in. bit to drill two clearance holes in each set of cross brace fixing guidelines.

Countersink all the cross brace fixing holes. This will ensure that all the screwheads are properly recessed in the panel uprights so that they will not snag on fingers or clothing once the screen has been assembled.

Take one set of panel uprights and cross braces and lay them on the workbench. Place the pieces squarely in position against each other. Drill ⅛ in. pilot holes into the ends of the cross braces through the panel upright clearance holes that you drilled in step 2. Use a thin layer of glue and No. 8 (2½ in.) screws to attach each cross brace to the two panel uprights. Ensure that all joints are square and even before drilling the screws firmly into place. Repeat the process with the other two sets of panel uprights and cross braces.

5 Take each assembled panel frame and fill any gaps and all screwheads using wood filler and a flexible filling knife. Wait for the filler to dry thoroughly and then use a sanding block and medium-grade abrasive paper to sand everything smooth. Pay particular attention to the areas around the joints where the cross braces meet the uprights.

6 The next step is to prepare the dowel fixing rods to which the screen canvas will be attached. Unroll the canvas on the workbench. Hold a length of dowel across it and mark a cut line to a width ¼ in. less than the width of the canvas (17¼ in.). Use a hand saw to cut 12 lengths of dowel—four for each panel—to the same length.

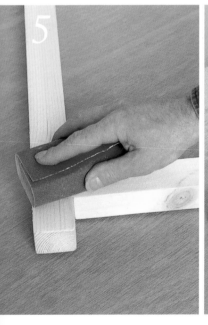

7 Place one of the assembled panel frames on the workbench. Roll out the canvas over the longest of the two sections of the panel. Allow 2 in. of fabric to protrude over the cross braces at each end of the section. Mark a cut line on the canvas roll at the bottom edge of the lower cross brace, as shown. Cut three pieces of canvas to the length marked.

8 Place one of the canvas lengths on the workbench. Cut a strip of double-sided tape to its width. Apply the tape strip along the bottom edge of the canvas and peel off the tape backing. Take one of the dowel fixing rods and fix it carefully in place on the sticky tape. Roll the protruding end of the canvas onto the dowel rod, as shown. Repeat the process at the other end of the canvas. Prepare the other two lengths of canvas that you cut in step 6 in the same way.

9 Use two G-clamps to clamp one of the lengths of canvas with attached dowel fixing rods to the longest section of one of the panel frames. Ensure that the canvas is taut in the panel section. Hold the panel upright on the workbench and drill three ½ in. pilot holes through the dowel fixing rod—one in the center and one at each end—and into the cross brace.

10 Use No. 6 (1 in.) round-headed screws to attach the dowel fixing rod and canvas to the cross brace. Repeat the process at the other end of the panel and for the other two panels that make up the screen. Repeat steps 6–10 to fix the remaining six dowel fixing rods and canvas into the shorter section of each panel frame. If you prefer, use a different colored canvas for these sections. Paint or varnish each of the panel frames according to your taste.

1 Measure and mark the positions of the hinges for attaching the three canvas panels together. Space them evenly on the panel uprights, 12 in. from each end. Attach the hinges to the panel uprights, using brass screws. Begin with the center panel first, attaching one hinge to the front-left edge of one panel upright and the other hinge to the back-right edge of the other upright, in order to effect an "accordion" fold in the screen as a whole.

2 Stand the three panels upright in order to attach them to one another with the hinges. Ensure that the panels are correctly aligned and completely square with one another before joining them together. Check that your accordion-fold effect works correctly across the three panels before securing them all together.

stencilling a
lampshade

It is easy to buy colorful lampshades, but not always quite so straightforward to find the particular pattern that you want. Taking a plain lampshade and stencilling it yourself overcomes this problem in an easy and economical way. This project shows you how to make a small floral stencil and then apply it to a plain lampshade. The technique can be used for any simple design, and if you wait for the paint to dry, you can also apply further colors or shapes.

Materials

1 medium-sized, plain lampshade • 1 piece of stencil card or mylar • Low-tack spray adhesive • Selection of acrylic or water-based paint colors

Tools

Work surface • Scalpel/craft knife • Cutting mat • 1 medium-sized white dinner plate • Pencil • 1 stencil brush • Masking tape • Roll of absorbent kitchen paper

Skill level

Beginner

Time

2 hours

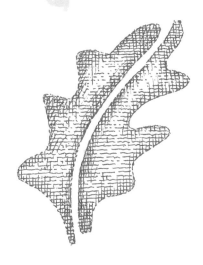

Easy home improvements

1 Copy the stencil template on page 110 of this book.
Draw your stencil pattern to the size that you want,
which will depend on the size of the lampshade that you
have selected for stencilling. Cut a square around your
drawing, leaving a clear margin of about 2 in. around the
actual outline of the leaf design. Cut out a square of
stencil card ½ in. larger than the square of your drawing.
Apply low-tack spray adhesive according to the
manufacturer's instructions, and press the pattern onto
the card, smoothing from the center outward.

2 Allow the adhesive to dry, then place the stencil card on
a piece of scrap plywood or a cutting mat. Cut out the
pattern of the leaf through the paper and the stencil
card, using a sharp hobby knife or scalpel. It is easier to
cut curves if you move the card to meet the blade
rather than the other way around.

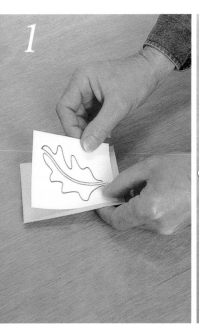

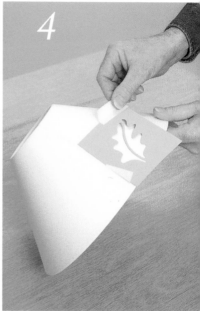

3   When you have cut smoothly around the outline of the
    design, ensuring that you cut all the way through the
    stencil card, carefully peel away the paper backing and
    cut-out pieces of card, as shown.

4   Take your lampshade and decide how you want to
    position each of your stencils on it. Hold the stencil up
    to the lampshade as you do this, to establish the best
    angles and positions to make the most of the design on
    the lampshade. When you are satisfied, use two short
    strips of masking tape to stick the stencil design onto
    the lampshade, ready to paint on the first pattern.

5 Squeeze out your selected acrylic or other water-based paint onto a clean, dry plate. Begin loading the stencil brush, just covering the ends of all the bristles, then dab most of the paint off onto absorbent kitchen paper, so that the brush is almost dry. Don't overload the brush.

6 Once you have gently secured the stencil card to the lampshade and prepared your paint, begin applying the pattern. Gently dab the paint onto the lampshade, through the cut-out stencil. Apply the paint by wiping the brush over the cutout in the stencil card, beginning at the edges and then filling in toward the center of the leaf. For a three-dimensional effect, add more paint to some areas of the leaf to darken it.

7 To apply the pattern to the edges of the lampshade, use masking tape to secure the design so that only part of the leaf will be visible on the edge of the lampshade. In this way, you can vary the pattern as you see fit.

8 Use a couple of pieces of absorbent kitchen paper to blot and wipe off the stencil card thoroughly between the applications of each leaf pattern. This will prevent any paint smudges from getting onto the lampshade. Repeat steps 6–8 until you have stencilled the entire lampshade. Allow the leaf stencils to dry thoroughly (because the paint is applied so sparingly, this will not take long), and your stencilled lampshade is ready for use.

stamp-printing
a wall

An imaginative and inexpensive way to decorate bare walls is to make a cut-out design from dense foam and then use it to stamp the designs on your wall. This design features a classical pattern that is particularly well-suited to bedroom walls, being light and soothing. The stamp is not difficult to make and the whole process is considerably easier to undertake than hanging wallpaper.

Materials

Dense foam—camping mat or similar type thick card (shoe box lid or other scrap) • Newspapers • Two different colors of acrylic paint

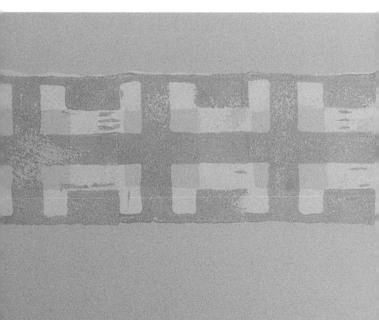

Tools

Spirit level • Tape measure • Scalpel/hobby knife and spare blades • Low-tack spray adhesive • Masking tape • Ball of string or reel of cotton • Small white dinner plate • 2 small foam rollers

Skill level

Intermediate

Time

4 hours

1 Trace the two patterns on page 110 of this book onto paper and enlarge them to the required sizes on a photocopier. Cut out two squares of paper to the required size and copy the designs onto them. Place the squares of paper over the sheet of foam and cut out two foam blocks to the same dimensions as the squares. Apply low-tack spray adhesive to stick the paper designs to the squares of foam. Begin cutting out the patterns using a scalpel or craft knife.

2 Cut around the outlines of the pattern shapes into the foam blocks to the depth of ¼ in. Make the cuts as evenly and cleanly as possible, ensuring that you do not press through to the bottom of the foam block. Nick off any extraneous pieces that obstruct a clean line.

Once you have cleanly cut around the designs, remove the paper templates and bend the foam blocks to open up the cut lines that you have made. Carefully use the craft knife to cut away the extraneous foam around the designs, leaving the designs raised in clear relief ¼ in. above the remaining bottom of the foam blocks.

Decide upon the positioning of the pattern on the wall. Secure a length of string or cotton at one corner of the wall with masking tape and run it along the wall to the opposite corner. Use a spirit level to check that the string is straight and perfectly horizontal.

5 Take a small dinner plate and squeeze some white acrylic paint onto it. Mix the white paint together with a small amount of whatever color is painted onto the wall you wish to stamp. This will ensure that the stamp will blend in harmoniously with the background color, creating a delicate, subtle, effect.

6 Use short strips of masking tape to fix little handles to the backs of the foam blocks that you cut out in steps 1–3. Make raised tape "loops" with which you can hold the foam blocks steady from behind. This will make it easier to stamp the wall later on. Run one of the foam rollers through the paint that you prepared in step 5, until it is evenly coated with paint all over. Then, run the roller over the "U"-shaped foam square. Ensure that the whole face of the foam square is evenly coated with paint.

7 Stamp the "U"-shaped pattern sideways onto the wall as shown, keeping the stamp lined up with the guide-string and butting each print up against the previous one. Press the back of the stamp with your fingers to ensure that the paint adheres evenly to the wall across the entire pattern.

8 Allow the paint to dry thoroughly. This will normally take a few hours. Take the second foam stamp and repeat steps 5–7. This time use a contrasting color of paint (we used ochre). Ensure that each second stamp pattern lines up accurately with the first ones, as shown.

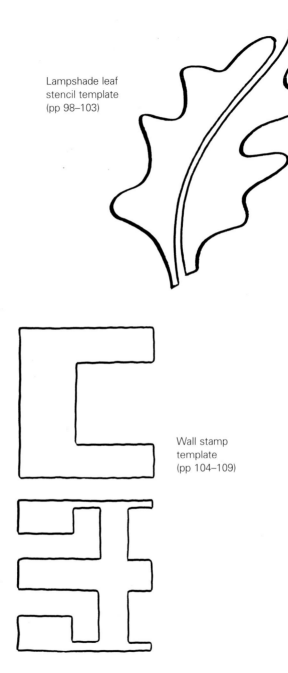

Lampshade leaf
stencil template
(pp 98–103)

Wall stamp
template
(pp 104–109)

glossary

Batten—a narrow strip of wood, often used to describe such a strip used as a support for other pieces

Countersink—to cut, usually drill, a hole that allows the head of a screw, nail, or pin to lie below the surface

MDF—medium-density fiberboard; a prefabricated material that can be worked like wood

Miter—a joint made by cutting equal angles, usually at 45 degrees to form a right angle in two pieces of wood; cutting such a joint

PAR—"planed all round;" timber that has been planed smooth on all sides

Pilot hole—a small-diameter hole drilled into wood to act as a guide for a screw thread

Stencil—a transferable ink or paint pattern

Template—a cut-out pattern on paper or cardboard, used to help shape wood or transfer a pattern (*cf.* stencil)

Upright—a vertical piece of wood, which is usually part of a frame

index

acknowledgments

All photographs taken by Alistair Hughes, except for:

8/9; 44/45 Elizabeth Whiting Associates; 70/71 Camera Press Ltd.

Illustrations by Stewart Walton.